THE CIRCULATORY SYSTEM

BY CONRAD J. STORAD

LERNER PUBLICATIONS COMPANY • MINNEAPOLIS

To my beautiful, wonderful stepdaughters: Sarah, the nurse, and Meghan, the teacher. Thank you for all the love and kindness you give to me and your mother.

The photographs in this book are used with the permission of: © Dr. David M. Phillips/Visuals Unlimited, pp. 5, 36 (bottom), 46; © Royalty-Free/CORBIS, pp. 6, 13, 15, 20, 24, 26, 48 (top); © Jim Cummins/CORBIS, p. 7; © Susumu Nishinaga/Photo Researchers, Inc., p. 8; © Dr. Gopal Murti/Visuals Unlimited, p. 9; © Gregg Otto/Visuals Unlimited, p. 10; © Stockbyte Royalty-Free, p. 11; © Kelly/Mooney Photography/CORBIS, p. 12; © Todd Strand/Independent Picture Service, pp. 14, 21, 25, 32; © SIU/Visuals Unlimited, pp. 16, 18; © Norbert Schaefer/ |CORBIS, p. 27; © Carolina Biological/Visuals Unlimited, pp. 28, 30; © L. Bassett/Visuals Unlimited, p. 31; © T. Kuwabara, D. W. Fawcett/Visuals Unlimited, p. 33; © Lester V. Bergman/ CORBIS, pp. 34, 43; © Beth Johnson/Independent Picture Service, p. 36 (top); © Photodisc Royalty Free by Getty Images, p. 38; © Dr. Richard Kessel & Dr. Gene Shih/Visuals Unlimited, p. 39; © Gladden Willis, M.D./Visuals Unlimited, p. 40; © Dr. Donald Fawcett & E. Shelton/ Visuals Unlimited, pp. 41, 48 (bottom); © Dr. Stanley Flegler/Visuals Unlimited, p. 42; © Francisco Cruz/SuperStock, p. 47.

Cover photograph © BSIP Agency/Index Stock Imagery.

Text copyright © 2005 by Conrad J. Storad

Lerner Publications Company
A division of Lerner Publishing Group
241 First Avenue North
Minneapolis, MN 55401 U.S.A

Website address: www.lernerbooks.com

Library of Congress Cataloging-in-Publication Data

Storad, Conrad J.
    The circulatory system / by Conrad J. Storad.
      p.   cm. — (Early bird body systems)
    Includes index.
    Summary: Describes the structure and function of the human circulatory system
    ISBN: 0–8225–1246–7 (lib. bdg. : alk. paper)
    1. Cardiovascular system—Juvenile literature. [1. Circulatory system.] I. Title. II. Series.
QP103.S76 2005
612.1—dc22   2003023003

Manufactured in the United States of America
1 2 3 4 5 6 – JR – 10 09 08 07 06 05

CONTENTS

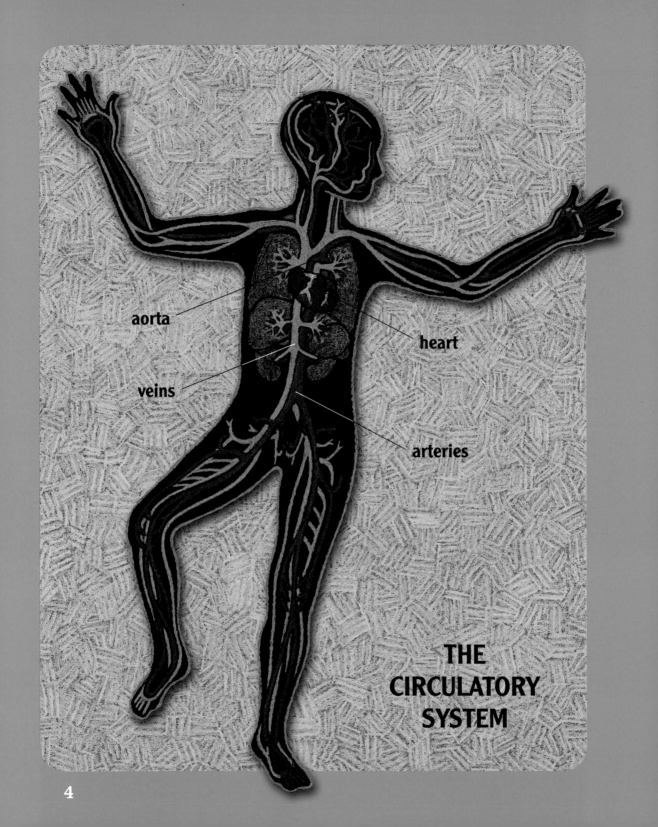

aorta

veins

heart

arteries

THE CIRCULATORY SYSTEM

BE A WORD DETECTIVE

Can you find these words as you read about the circulatory system? Be a detective and try to figure out what they mean. You can turn to the glossary on page 46 for help.

arteries   clot   valves
atrium   hemoglobin   veins
blood   oxygen   ventricle
blood vessels   plasma   white blood cells
capillaries   platelets
carbon dioxide   red blood cells

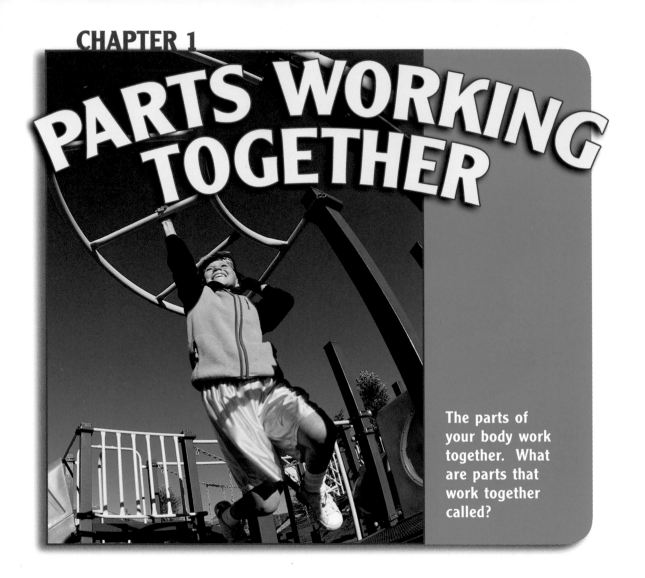

CHAPTER 1

PARTS WORKING TOGETHER

The parts of your body work together. What are parts that work together called?

Each part of the body has a job. The parts work together. Parts that work together are called a system.

The body has many systems. One system helps the body turn food into energy. Another

6

system helps the body breathe. Another helps the body to move.

One important body system is called the circulatory system. This system's job is to pump blood to all parts of the body.

Without your circulatory system, you wouldn't be able to climb, jump, or run.

The circulatory system is made up of the heart, the blood, and many strong tubes called blood vessels (VEH-suhlz). The heart makes the blood move through the blood vessels. Blood vessels carry the blood to all parts of the body.

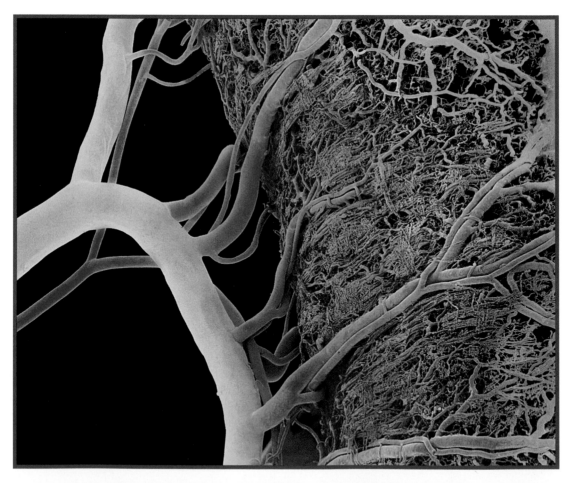

Blood vessels are tubes that carry blood to all parts of the body.

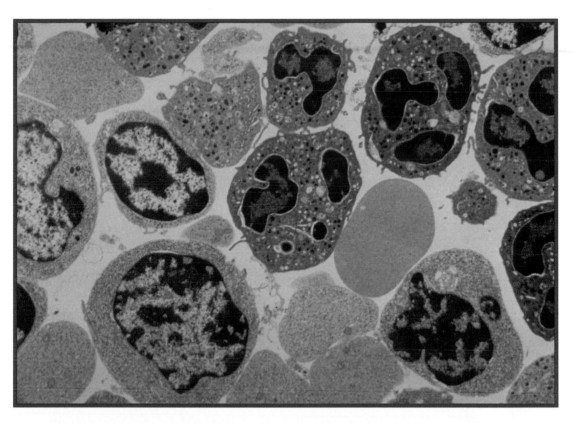

Your body is made of millions of tiny cells. A microscope was used to take this picture of cells from inside a bone.

All body parts are made of cells. Cells are so small you need a microscope to see them. The human body has many different kinds of cells. It has muscle cells and bone cells. It has skin cells and brain cells. It has nerve cells and blood cells.

Your body breaks down everything you eat or drink. Then your blood carries the food to your cells.

Every cell needs food to live. Food goes into the blood each time we eat or drink. Every cell also needs oxygen (AHK-suh-jehn). Oxygen is a gas in the air. Oxygen goes into the blood every time we take a breath. The blood carries food and oxygen to every cell.

10

Cells make waste as they do their jobs. The blood collects the waste and carries it away. Carbon dioxide is one kind of waste that cells make. Carbon dioxide is a kind of gas. The blood carries carbon dioxide from the cells to the lungs. We get rid of carbon dioxide every time we breathe out. Cells also make other kinds of waste. The body gets rid of these kinds of waste every time we go to the bathroom.

When you breathe out, you get rid of carbon dioxide.

CHAPTER 2

THE HEART

Your heart never stops pumping blood. What is your heart made of?

The heart has a big job to do. The heart pumps blood to all parts of the body. It pumps blood every second. It pumps blood every day and every night.

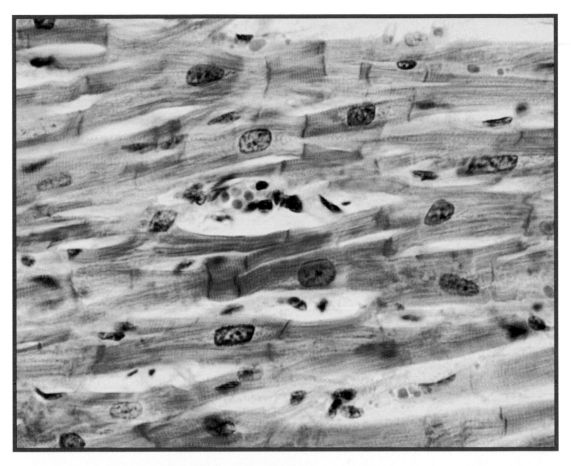

Heart muscle cells are long and thin.

The heart can pump blood because it is made of muscle. The muscles in your arms and legs make your bones move. The muscle in your heart squeezes to pump blood through your body.

The heart works hard. But it is not very big.
Your heart is about the same size as your fist.

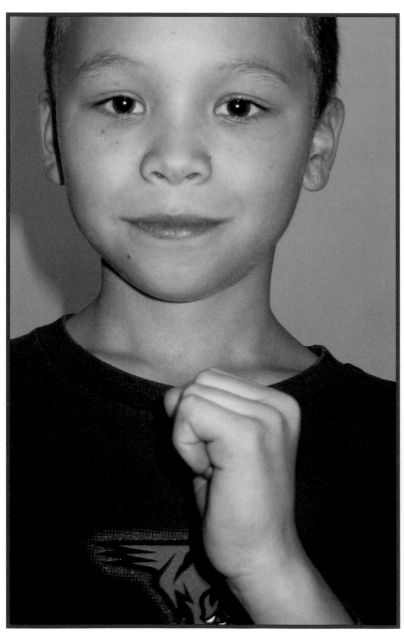

**Your heart is
about the same
size as your fist.**

Your heart beats on its own. You don't have to think about making it pump blood. So you can think about other things, like schoolwork.

The heart pumps blood when we eat. It pumps blood when we sleep. It pumps blood when we exercise. It never rests.

In the middle of the heart is a thick wall of muscle. This wall is called the septum. The septum separates the heart into a right half and a left half. The septum stops blood from leaking from one side of the heart to the other.

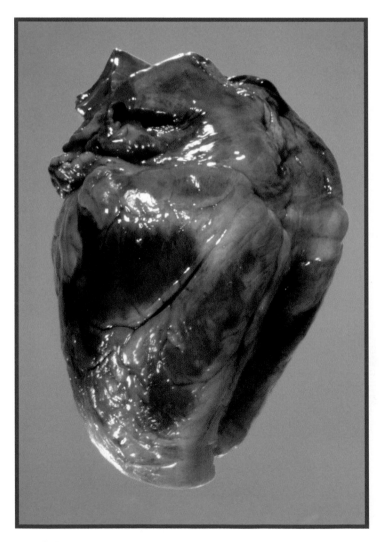

An adult's heart weighs only about 10 ounces. That is a little more than an orange weighs.

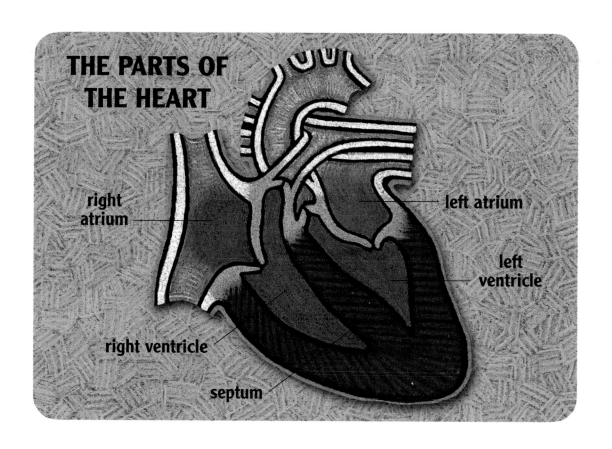

THE PARTS OF THE HEART

right atrium

left atrium

left ventricle

right ventricle

septum

Each half of the heart is made up of two hollow rooms. The rooms are stacked one on top of the other. Each top room is called an atrium (AY-tree-uhm). There is a right atrium and a left atrium. Each bottom room is called a ventricle. There is a right ventricle and a left ventricle. As the heart pumps blood, the blood moves through each of these rooms.

Blood always moves in the same direction through the heart. It moves from the left atrium into the left ventricle. It moves from the right atrium into the right ventricle. It cannot go backward.

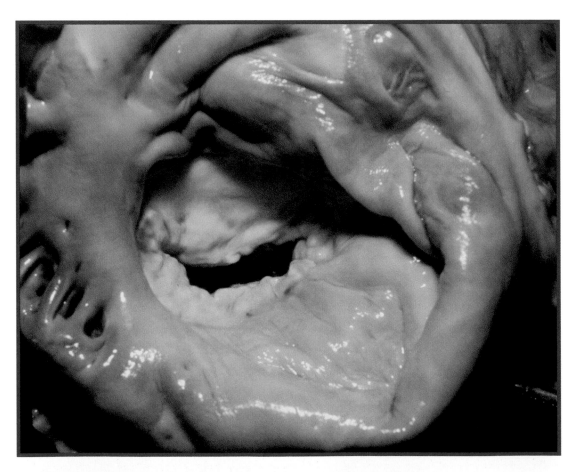

Flaps of muscle shut to keep blood from moving backward through the heart.

HOW A HEART VALVE WORKS

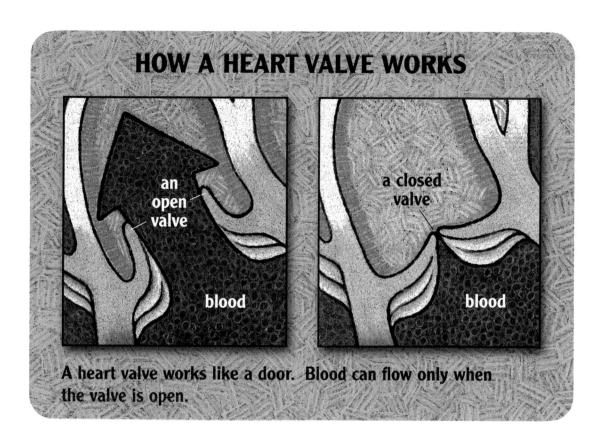

an open valve

blood

a closed valve

blood

A heart valve works like a door. Blood can flow only when the valve is open.

Each half of the heart has special flaps made of muscle. The flaps separate the atrium from the ventricle. These flaps are called valves. Each valve is like a door. It opens only one way. When the valve opens, blood flows from the atrium to the ventricle. Then the valve closes quickly. It does not let the blood flow back into the atrium.

On the outside wall of each ventricle is another valve. When the ventricles are full of blood, these valves open. The blood flows from the ventricles into the blood vessels. Then the valves close again.

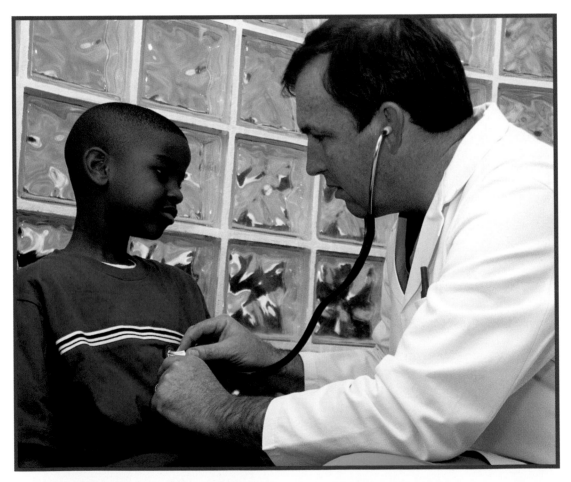

Doctors listen to the heart to make sure it is working well.

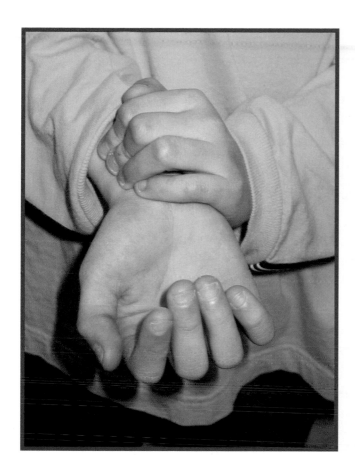

Press your fingertips tightly against the inside of your wrist. Can you feel the blood pumping?

The heart makes a sound each time its valves close. That sound is called a heartbeat. It sounds like *lub-DUB, lub-DUB, lub-DUB.*

The right side of the heart pumps blood to the lungs. The left side of the heart pumps blood to the rest of the body. The heart squeezes hard each time it pumps the blood.

The heart beats over and over and over again. It always beats in the same way. First the heart relaxes. Blood pours into the left atrium. This blood comes from the lungs. It carries lots of oxygen. At exactly the same time, blood fills the right atrium. This blood came from the body's cells. It does not have much oxygen.

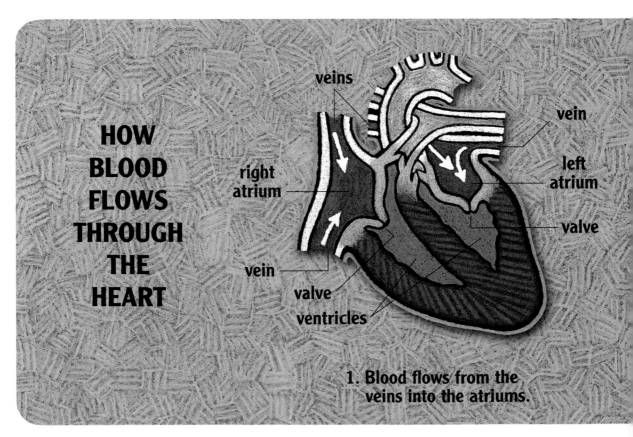

HOW BLOOD FLOWS THROUGH THE HEART

veins

vein

right atrium

left atrium

valve

vein

valve

ventricles

1. Blood flows from the veins into the atriums.

The valves inside the heart open. The heart muscle squeezes. Blood from the atriums is pushed down into the ventricles. The valves snap shut. *Lub.*

Next, the valves on the outside of the ventricles open. The heart muscle squeezes. Blood is pushed out of the ventricles and into the blood vessels. The valves snap shut. *DUB.*

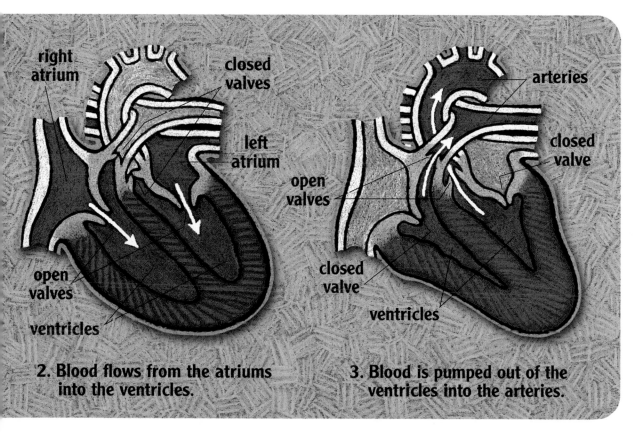

2. Blood flows from the atriums into the ventricles.

3. Blood is pumped out of the ventricles into the arteries.

The right ventricle pushes blood to the lungs. There, the blood collects oxygen. Then it travels back toward the heart.

The left ventricle pushes blood out to all of the rest of the body. It pumps blood to the top of our heads and to the tips of our toes.

Your heart is strong. It can pump blood high above your head.

People faint if their brain cells don't get enough oxygen. If you feel wobbly and strange, try sitting with your head down. This helps your heart pump lots of blood and oxygen to your brain.

Blood from the left ventricle carries lots of oxygen. The blood delivers the oxygen to the body's cells. Then the blood travels back to the heart. The right ventricle will pump it to the lungs to get more oxygen.

CHAPTER 3

BLOOD VESSELS

Blood vessels carry blood through the body. How many kinds of blood vessels are there?

Blood is always moving through the body. The blood moves in two big circles. One circle runs from the heart to the lungs and back again. The other circle runs from the heart to the rest of the body and back to the heart.

The blood travels through the blood vessels. Some blood vessels are big. Others are tiny. There are three different kinds of blood vessels.

HOW THE HEART PUMPS BLOOD THROUGH THE BODY

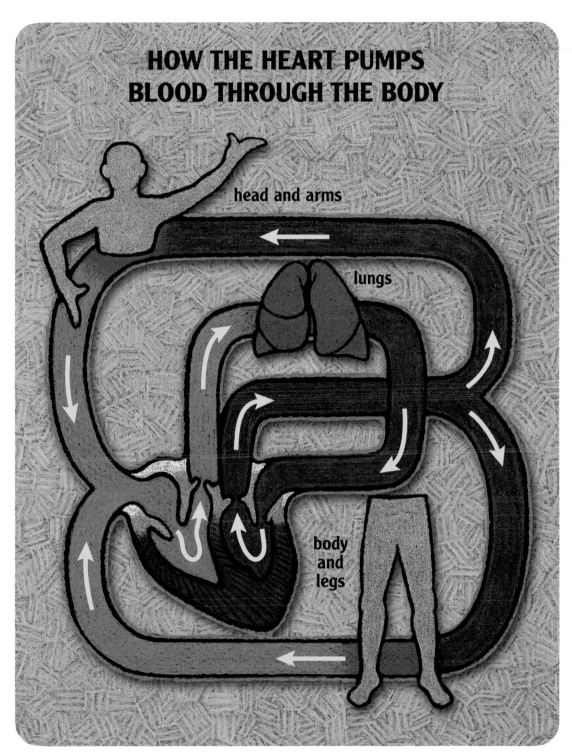

head and arms

lungs

body
and
legs

The strongest blood vessels are called arteries (AHR-tuh-reez). Arteries have thick, strong walls. They carry blood away from the heart. Arteries carry blood to all parts of the body.

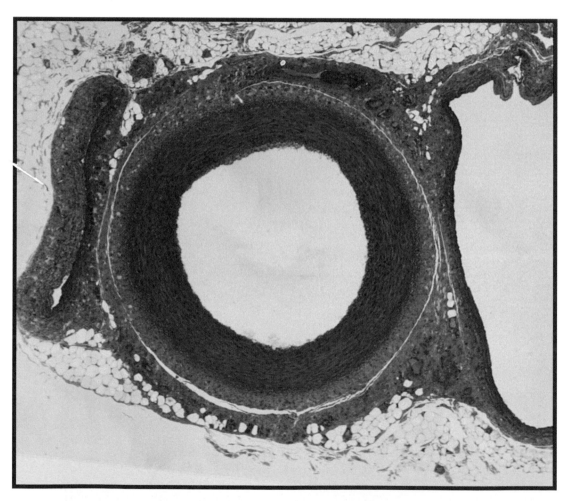

This picture shows the thick walls of an artery. The walls are made of strong muscle.

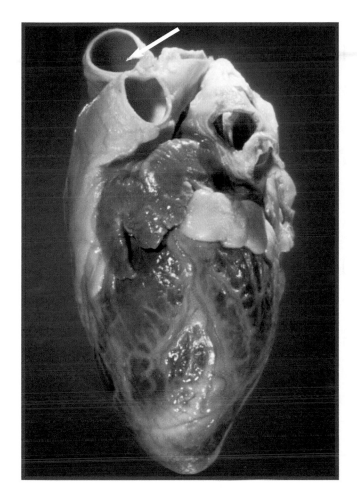

The arrow shows where the aorta connects to the heart.

The biggest artery is called the aorta (ay-OR-tuh). An adult's aorta is almost as wide as a quarter. The aorta is connected to the left ventricle. Smaller arteries branch off of the aorta. As the blood travels further and farther from the heart, the arteries get smaller and smaller.

Veins (VAYNZ) are the second kind of blood vessel. Veins have strong walls. But they are not as strong as arteries. Veins carry blood back to the heart. Blood in some of the veins carries waste from the cells. It does not have much oxygen. Other veins carry blood from the lungs. This blood has a lot of oxygen that is ready to be delivered to the cells.

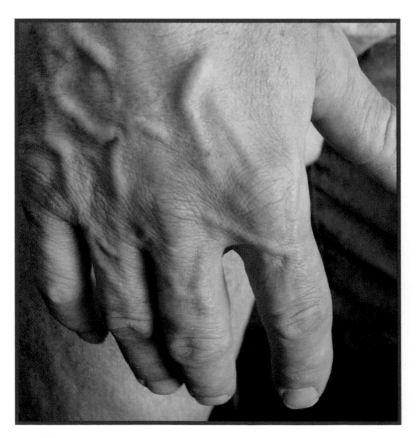

You can see veins just under the skin of this man's hand.

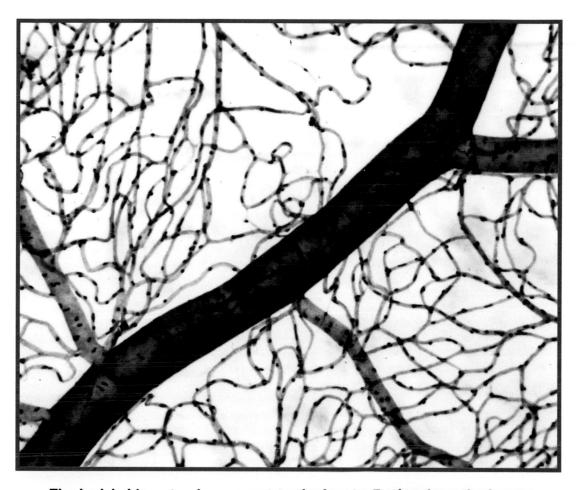

The body's biggest veins connect to the heart. Farther from the heart, veins are smaller.

An adult's biggest veins are about as wide as a pencil. These veins are attached to the heart's atriums. Veins that are farther away from the heart are smaller.

The smallest blood vessels are called capillaries (CAP-uh-LAY-reez). Capillaries connect the smallest arteries to the smallest veins. The capillaries are very important. They carry blood to every single cell in the body.

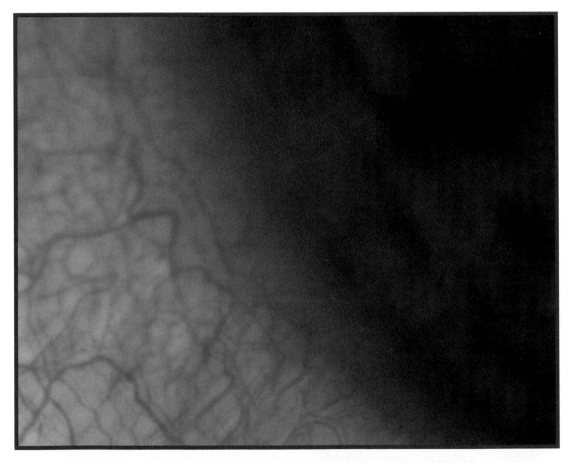

This is a close-up picture of part of a person's eye. The red lines are capillaries.

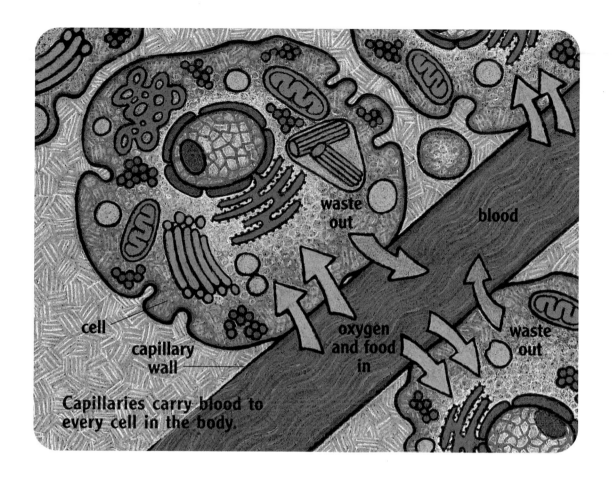

waste out

blood

cell

capillary wall

oxygen and food in

waste out

Capillaries carry blood to every cell in the body.

Capillaries are tiny. They have very thin walls. Food, oxygen, and waste can go right through the capillaries' thin walls. Food and oxygen go from the blood into the cells. The cells push waste out into the capillaries. The capillaries carry blood loaded with waste back to the veins so the body can get rid of it.

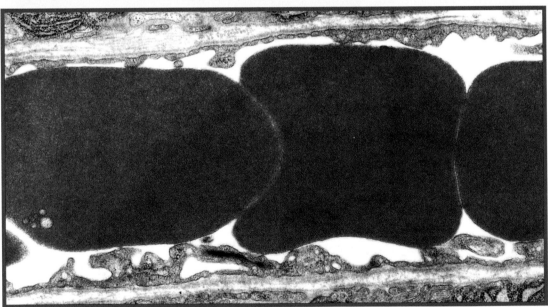

TOP: Exercise makes some people's cheeks turn pink. The pink color comes from blood in capillaries just under the skin.
BOTTOM: Capillaries are tiny. Blood cells are squeezed as they move through capillaries.

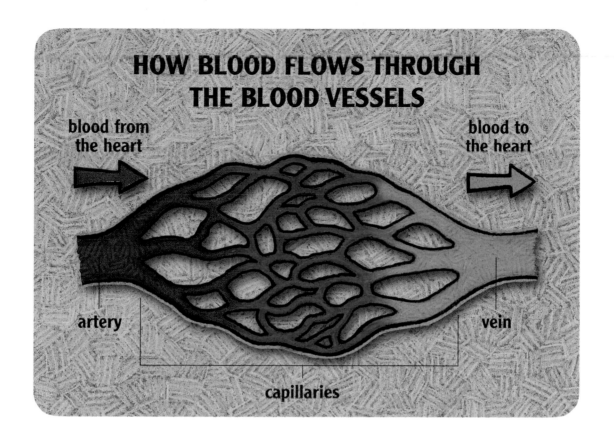

HOW BLOOD FLOWS THROUGH THE BLOOD VESSELS

blood from the heart

blood to the heart

artery

vein

capillaries

Blood travels through the body over and over. The blood flows from the heart into the arteries. The arteries carry the blood to capillaries in all parts of the body. The blood flows from the capillaries into the veins. Then the veins carry the blood back to the heart. The blood takes this trip over and over again, every minute of every day.

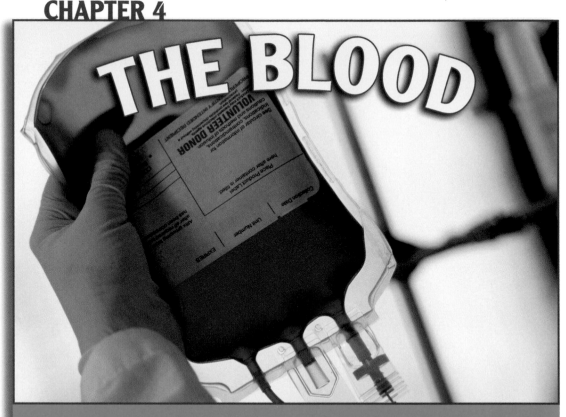

CHAPTER 4

A person who is sick or hurt may need more blood. Other people can help by sharing some of their blood. Why is blood red?

Blood has lots of different parts. There are red blood cells, white blood cells, and platelets (PLATE-lets). All of these parts float in a clear liquid called plasma (PLAZ-muh). Most of the cells floating in the plasma are red blood cells. That is why our blood is red.

Red blood cells look like doughnuts with no hole in the middle.

Red blood cells look like flat, red doughnuts. Red blood cells contain a chemical called hemoglobin (HEE-muh-GLO-bihn). Oxygen sticks to hemoglobin. Hemoglobin helps blood carry oxygen to the body's cells.

The body has millions of red blood cells. These cells live for only a short time. But the body is always making new red blood cells. Red blood cells are made inside of our bones.

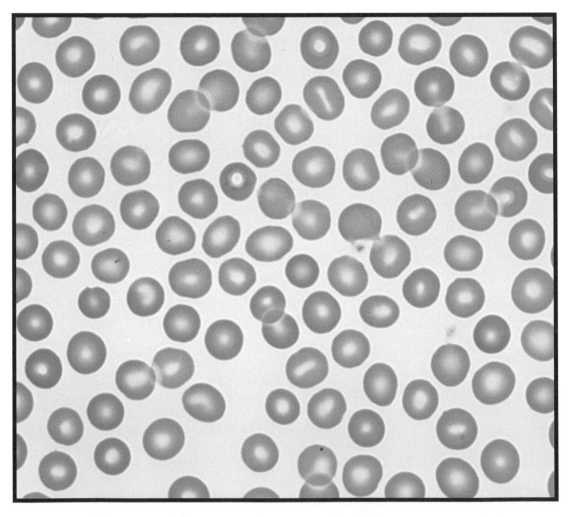

Red blood cells live for about three to four months.

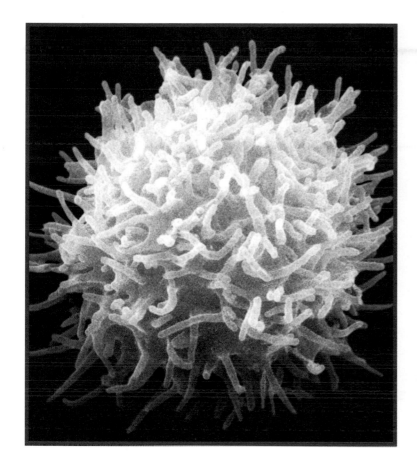

White blood cells look like bumpy, white balls.

There are not as many white blood cells as red blood cells. But white blood cells are still very important. White blood cells are like guards in the blood. They protect the body from things that might make us sick. White blood cells gobble up germs and other bad things that get into our blood.

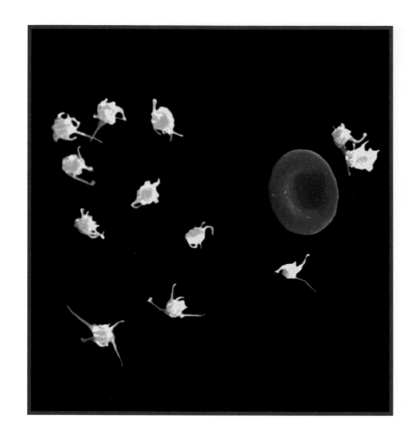

Platelets are much smaller than red blood cells.

Blood also has tiny parts called platelets. Platelets help the body to fix itself.

If we get hurt, blood vessels may get cut or broken. Blood can leak out through a hole in a blood vessel. The hole has to be closed. Platelets in the blood stick to the edges of the hole. More and more platelets pile up in the hole. The platelets tell red blood cells to clump together over the hole. The cells form a hard clump called a clot. The clot plugs the hole and stops blood from flowing out through it.

Blood is an important part of the circulatory system. But it is just one part. The blood needs the heart. The heart needs the blood vessels. All of the parts work together to keep us alive.

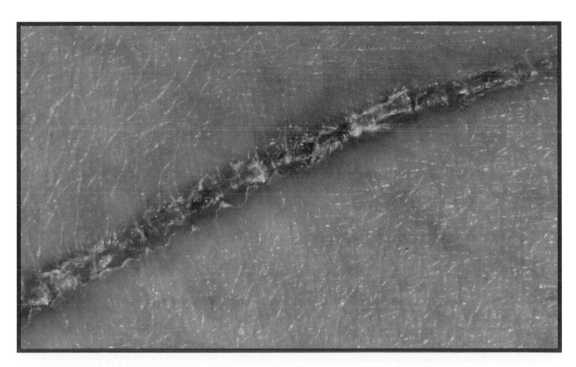

Platelets and red blood cells work together to stop bleeding and help cuts to heal.

ON SHARING A BOOK

When you share a book with a child, you show that reading is important. To get the most out of the experience, read in a comfortable, quiet place. Turn off the television and limit other distractions, such as telephone calls.

Be prepared to start slowly. Take turns reading parts of this book. Stop occasionally and discuss what you're reading. Talk about the photographs. If the child begins to lose interest, stop reading. When you pick up the book again, revisit the parts you have already read.

BE A VOCABULARY DETECTIVE

The word list on page 5 contains words that are important in understanding the topic of this book. Be word detectives and search for the words as you read the book together. Talk about what the words mean and how they are used in the sentence. Do any of these words have more than one meaning? You will find the words defined in a glossary on page 46.

WHAT ABOUT QUESTIONS?

Use questions to make sure the child understands the information in this book. Here are some suggestions:

> What did this paragraph tell us? What does this picture show? What do you think we'll learn about next? What does the circulatory system do? How big is your heart? Why does your heart beat faster when you exercise? What are the three kinds of blood vessels? What is blood made up of? What is your favorite part of the book? Why?

If the child has questions, don't hesitate to respond with questions of your own, such as What do *you* think? Why? What is it that you don't know? If the child can't remember certain facts, turn to the index.

INTRODUCING THE INDEX

The index helps readers find information without searching through the whole book. Turn to the index on page 47. Choose an entry such as *red blood cells* and ask the child to use the index to find out where red blood cells are made. Repeat with as many entries as you like. Ask the child to point out the differences between an index and a glossary. (The index helps readers find information, while the glossary tells readers what words mean.)

LEARN MORE ABOUT
THE CIRCULATORY SYSTEM

BOOKS

Frost, Helen. *The Circulatory System.* Mankato, MN: Pebble Books, 2001. Introduces the circulatory system, its purpose, parts, and functions.

Gray, Susan Heinrichs. *The Circulatory System.* Chanhassen, MN: Child's World, 2004. This book gives clear, vivid explanations of how the circulatory system works.

Royston, Angela. *Why Do Bruises Change Color?: And Other Questions About Blood.* Chicago, IL: Heinemann Library, 2003. How does blood move through the body? Why do your hands and feet get cold first? Find out the answers to these and other questions about blood.

Stille, Darlene R. *The Circulatory System.* New York: Children's Press, 1997. Describes the parts of the human circulatory system and explains how and why blood is circulated throughout the body.

WEBSITES

Circulatory System
< http://hes.ucf.k12.pa.us/gclaypo/circulatorysys.html>
This website has circulatory system facts and diagrams and an animation of how blood flows through the heart.

My Body
<http://www.kidshealth.org/kid/body/mybody.html>
This fun website has information on the systems of the human body, plus movies, games, and activities.

Pathfinders for Kids: The Circulatory System — The Life Pump
< http://infozone.imcpl.org/kids_circ.htm >
This web page has a list of resources you can use to learn more about the circulatory system.

GLOSSARY

arteries (AHR-tuh-reez): tubes that carry blood away from the heart

atrium (AY-tree-uhm): one of the top rooms in the heart

blood: the red liquid that the heart pumps through the body

blood vessels (VEH-suhlz): the tubes in the body through which blood flows

capillaries (CAP-uh-LAY-reez): tiny blood vessels that connect the smallest arteries to the smallest veins

carbon dioxide: a gas that is one kind of waste that cells make

clot: a hard clump of platelets and red blood cells

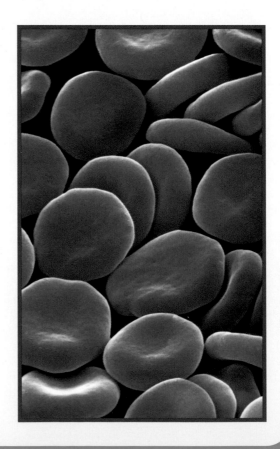

hemoglobin (HEE-muh-GLO-bihn): a chemical in red blood cells. Hemoglobin helps the blood carry oxygen to the body's cells.

oxygen (AHK-suh-jehn): a gas in the air that cells need

plasma (PLAZ-muh): the liquid part of blood. Blood cells and platelets float in the plasma.

platelets (PLATE-lets): tiny parts of the blood that help the body to fix itself

red blood cells: cells in the blood that carry oxygen. Red blood cells look like flat, red doughnuts.

valves: flaps of muscle that keep blood from flowing backward through the heart

veins (VAYNZ): tubes that carry blood toward the heart

ventricle: one of the bottom rooms in the heart

white blood cells: cells that protect the body from things that might make us sick

INDEX

Pages listed in **bold** type refer to photographs.

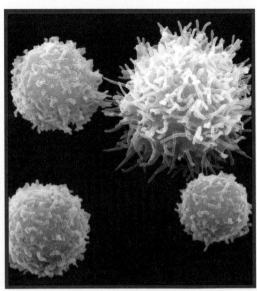